GW00456616

ISBN 9798489592819

 thelittlebookoficks@gmail.com

@thelittlebookoficks

THE
LITTLE
BOOK
OF
ICKS

We asked the nation what their 'Icks' were. Some responses were funny, some were gross, and some were down right outrageous. Whether you're guilty of being turned off within minutes of the first date, or you're the one making your Hinge match's stomach turn, you can find solace in these stories. Here's to modern dating, in all of its messy, magical, mind-fucking glory.

"Ick"

We've all felt it. That unmistakable feeling which creeps up out of nowhere and takes over you mid-date. The sudden burning sensation of pure cringe which turns any seemingly normal, sweet, or even endearing behaviour into something so toe-curl-ingly revolting even Satan would stir in his grave: the Ick. It usually rears its ugly head at the early stages of a relationship or situationship – once you have it, you're done for. Everything will be going fine – great, even – then, before you know it, an overwhelming feeling of disgust turns those butterflies in your stomach into overwhelming, gut-wrenching cringe.

This short yet powerful three letter word explains the feelings behind your decision to leave your date sitting alone at the conveyor belt at Yo! Sushi, ghost their calls, or pack it in altogether. No-one is safe from the Ick. The guy from halls you've fancied since first year? Nope. Your brother's best friend who always smells nice? No. The dreamy Hinge date who took you out for dinner, drinks, AND paid for the Uber home? Not even him. You could contract the Ick for no apparent reason, but once it's happened... there's no going back.

01 JUMPING THE GUN

"I once went on a date with an older guy who kept telling me he couldn't wait to take me home to visit his 'Mama'... He kept trying to hold my hands across the table and stroke them, then dropped several hints that he had upgraded his joint hostel room to a private single room. I ordered the Uber home while he was still sipping his drink, and blocked his number as soon as I stepped foot in the car."

02 CHOCOLATE DUSTINGS

"There was a guy I had slept with a couple times (mind-blowing stuff) and was very smitten with... all until he took me for coffee for our third date. Everything was going well until I noticed the chocolate dustings from his cappuccino had gathered at the sides of his mouth. I couldn't focus on anything else. I didn't even have the decency to tell him - I could only look on in disgust. The choccy dustings combined with his deathly coffee breath had me eyeing up the illuminated emergency exit sign like it was the gateway to heaven."

03 DESIGNER CLOTHES

"My ex used to lay out his designer clothes on his bed, making sure I was aware of his 'Ralphs', Hugos' and 'Monclers'. Made. Me. Shudder. And before you ask – yes, he was compensating for something."

04 NO BALANCE

"Eyeing up potentials on the Northern Line home and seeing one or two unfortunate souls losing, and quickly trying to regain their balance. Any remaining glimmer of seductive eye contact has now been shattered. Why not just hold onto the railings?!"

05 THE CHANT

"Imagine a man taking you to a rugby game and shouting 'oggy, oggy, oggy', only to be met with deafening silence, with him sitting there awkwardly laughing off the shame... I feel this cringe in my very soul."

06 HOT COFFEE

"Holding a steaming hot coffee with two hands like a 45 year old woman sipping hot cocoa on her deck whilst wearing shawl... eek".

07 UNEXPECTED SERENADE

"Nothing freaks me out more than someone suddenly breaking out in song. Double cringe points awarded if painfully intense eye contact is maintained throughout their pitchy, unexpected and unwanted rendition of 'Perfect' by Ed Sheeran. If they whip out a musical instrument to accompany their warblings (think acoustic guitar or ukulele), then run."

08 BREAKFAST IS SERVED

"I had recently started seeing someone, and it was Valentine's Day only three weeks into us dating – which was awkward anyway. They decided to surprise me with breakfast in bed, which was pretty cute. Unfortunately, they walked in with the tray while announcing 'brekkie is served!'. Pretty sure it made the milk in my tea curdle. I really had to work hard to overlook that one."

09 DOGGY DAYCARE

"I cannot stand the words 'doggo', 'pupper', or 'woofer' when someone is talking about a dog. It is not cute, and you are not four years old. Ten times worse if they use a baby voice when exclaiming 'what a good doggo!' upon seeing a smelly old labrador."

10 RAINY DAY

"Painfully watching a man furiously wrestle with his umbrella as it is repeatedly blown inside out by the wind...enough said."

11 ALL FOURS

"Whenever my friends can't quite seem to get over someone, I always tell them to think of their ex running up the stairs on all fours. Imagining a fully grown adult bounding up the stairs while panting in exertion usually does it for me."

12 DANGLING LEGS

"I have nothing against short men, but when a man's legs don't reach the floor when they sit on a bar stool, I feel incredibly uneasy. Sitting there, sipping your beer with your legs dangling in the air... please no."

13 TRAMPOLINE TERROR

"My man used to enjoy being the one who would curl up into a ball in order to be the 'egg' during a game of the trampoline craze "crack the egg". This will forever be one of my worst memories."

14 SIT BACK & ENJOY THE SHOW

"As a student in Edinburgh, I once went on a first date to a Fringe Festival show. It seemed like a good idea at the time – if the chat was dead, we could always sit quietly and watch the show, as well as have something in common to discuss after. Well let me tell you, when my date was practically begging to get involved during an audience participation opportunity, I was ready to hide under my seat. To make matters worse, it was a magic show. I swiftly chugged my £8 glass of wine whilst watching him climb into a box for the magician to 'make him disappear'. Any chance of a second date vanished simultaneously."

COME AND SEE THE SHOW

THE MOST EMBARASSING DATE EVER

15 PING PONG GONE WRONG

"I thought I liked activity dates until I had to watch him run after a ping pong ball which went awry. It was humiliating for us both, to be fair..."

16 BARBERSHOP BOOST

"Watching my man getting boosted up on the chair at the barbers during his haircut really put me off him for a couple of days. Seeing his little head bumping further and further up in the mirror whilst wearing that cape... nah. Not for me."

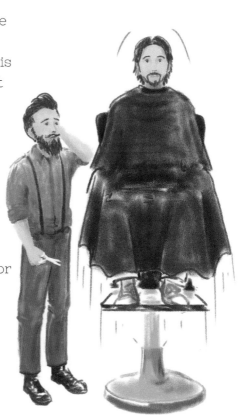

17 CONFIDENTLY WRONG

"I matched with a guy on Hinge. I then saw his Instagram story – he was sat erect in an IKEA office chair singing 'Wild Thoughts', while he made continuous (and uncomfortable) eye contact as he pointed at the camera. This in itself was harrowing, but he went one step further and got the vast majority of the words wrong. He decided to upload the recording anyway. I locked my phone and threw it across the room. I have aired every DM he has sent me since..."

18 KISS ME THRU THE PHONE

"Anyone who uses any form of the monkey emoji - especially following a text like 'hey cutie', or responding to a thirst trap. Just no."

19 SMELLS LIKE NO SECOND DATE

"I once went on a date with a guy who I could smell before he even reached the table. Even worse, he was a 'where's my hug?' type. I held my breath as he went for it but the pungent smell of BO assaulted my nostrils and lingered for the remainder of the date. I just wanted to die."

20 MUMMY ISSUES

"Calling your mum 'mummy'/'mama'. You're 27, not 7. You either have mummy issues or haven't yet grown up. Either way: red flag. The same goes for kissing your mum on the mouth; regardless of how close they are, it doesn't sit well in my spirit. Am I about to be a side chick/compete with your mum?"

21 PEDICURE PENDING

"I was with a guy a few years ago and couldn't spot a single flaw. He seemed amazing, and so was the sex. This remained the case until one evening in bed when I felt something sharp scraping at my ankles. I took a look when I got up and went to the toilet.

I almost collapsed when I saw that he had crusty, yellowing, long-ass wolverine toenails. I had to give myself a pep talk in the bathroom just to go back in."

22 BOTTOMS UP

"Something about seeing a guy's bare arse the morning after is so shameful. I cannot see your bum cheeks. The same goes for seeing your bum crack as you get out of the car. No. Thank. You."

23 STRAW SEARCHING

"A date took me to a burger bar. It was our fourth or fifth date so things were a bit more relaxed by this point. That was until he became so enticed by our conversation that he refused to drop eye contact, choosing to soul search for his straw with his tongue instead."

24 L'ADDITION S'IL VOUS PLAÎT

"As ridiculous as this sounds, if someone is ignored after asking for the bill as a waiter or waitress walks past, I feel overcome with shame."

25 SHOE HORN

"Watching him wrestle his trotters into his new Churches by waggling the shoe horn from left to right. The worst part is him gasping in relief when he finally squeezes them in."

26 MIRROR, MIRROR ON THE WALL

"If I see any kind of mirror selfie, pouty or not, you will be punished with a 'swipe left'. The mirror is usually dusty or dirty, or splattered with toothpaste marks. Yuck."

27 TIGHT FISTED

"Tight guys – enough said. He takes you for dinner and opts for the cheapest thing on the menu and then has the audacity to try and tempt you with the side salad when really your heart is calling out for the lobster linguine. In for a penny, in for a pound. Double ew if he whips out his Unidays or tries to pay with coupons."

28 SKID MARKS

"I had gone on a couple dates with a guy, and he invited me over to his place so he could cook me dinner. Everything was going well – the wine was flowing, food was banging, and the sexual tension was through the roof. I excused myself to go to the toilet, but what I saw made me feel like throwing up the spag bol he had so lovingly made: skids on the toilet bowl! They looked fresh too – not that I examined them... I felt myself burning with shame – what if he thought they were mine? This man is surely not going to have me scrubbing HIS poo off HIS toilet?!

I felt ill every time he tried to put his hands on me. Never spoke to him again."

29 OVERLY EXCITABLE

"I find there to be nothing worse than a bloke who is overly excitable. Sit down and play the cool and sophisticated card."

30 CTRL ALT DELETE

"Don't get me wrong, the desire to get the work done is sexy. God I love a driven man, but that posture, hunched over, knees touching, laptop balancing, suffocates all. Ctrl Alt Delete."

Printed in Great Britain
by Amazon